VOCAL SELECTIONS FROM

Walt Disney's Peter Pan

ISBN 0-88188-414-6

HAL•LEONARD® CORPORATION

7777 W. BLUEMOUND RD. P.O. BOX 13819 MILWAUKEE, WI 53213

Contents

You Can Fly! You Can Fly! You Can Fly!

Words by SAMMY CAHN
Music by SAMMY FAIN

Moderately

Think of the pres-ents you've brought
When there's a smile in your heart
An - y mer-ry lit - tle thought
There's no bet - ter time to start

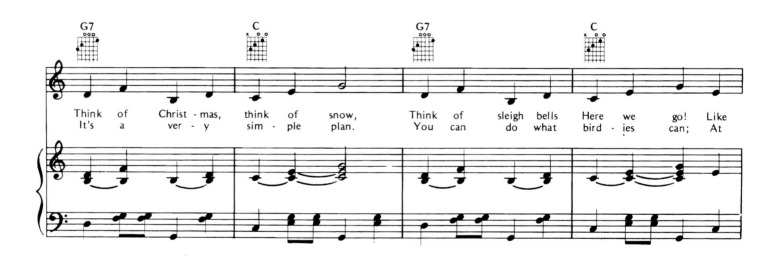

Think of Christ - mas, think of snow,
It's a ver - y sim - ple plan.
Think of sleigh bells Here we go! Like
You can do what bird - ies go! can; At

rein - deer in the sky
least it's worth a try
You can fly! You can

To Coda ⊕

The Second Star To The Right

Words by SAMMY CAHN
Music by SAMMY FAIN

The sec - ond star to the right shines in the night for
The sec - ond star to the right shines with a light that's

you
rare,
to tell you that the dreams you plan
and if it's Nev - er Land you need, its

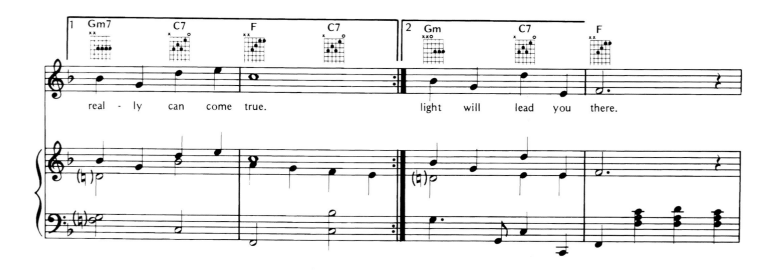

1. real - ly can come true.
2. light will lead you there.

The Elegant Captain Hook

Words by SAMMY CAHN
Music by SAMMY FAIN

It is Wendy Darling's last night in the nursery bedroom. Her father George says it's time for her to grow up and stop telling wild stories about Peter Pan, the boy who never grew up, to her younger brothers, John and Michael.

Not long after George and his wife Mary leave for a London party, Peter Pan himself flies through the nursery window. He is looking for his lost shadow, which Wendy found and then hid away.

When Wendy awakens to find Peter trying vainly to attach the shadow to his feet, she stitches it back on for him.

Peter Pan offers to take Wendy to his island, where she can tell fabulous stories and be a mother to his followers (or "band"), The Lost Boys. Wendy awakens John and Michael. With happy thoughts and some pixie dust from Tinker Bell, Peter's sprite friend, the three Darlings learn to fly and head for Never Land. They leave behind Nana, their dog and nursemaid, who can only fly to the end of her tether.

You Can Fly! You Can Fly! You Can Fly!

As Peter and the children survey the island from a cloud, Captain Hook, Peter's one-handed archenemy, fires a cannon at them from his pirate ship. Ordering Tinker Bell to take the others to safety. Peter stays behind to playfully draw away Hook's fire.

The Elegant Captain Hook

Jealous of the way Peter treats Wendy, Tinker Bell rushes ahead and rouses the Lost Boys, telling them that Peter has ordered them to shoot down the terrible Wendy Bird. Using slingshots, they knock Wendy from the sky, but Peter flies in and catches her just before she crashes to the ground. Angry, Peter charges Tinker Bell with treason and banishes her from the island for a week.

While Peter takes Wendy to Mermaid Lagoon, John and Michael stay to fight Indians with the Lost Boys. The Indians surround and capture them. The chief tells them they won't be released until they disclose the whereabouts of the beautiful Indian Princess, Tiger Lily.

What Made The Red Man Red?

None of the boys can tell the Indians where to find their princess, but meanwhile, in Mermaid Lagoon, Peter and Wendy see Hook and his first mate, Mr. Smee, take Tiger Lily into Skull Rock. There, the captain demands that the princess reveal the location of Peter Pan's hideout. She refuses, and Peter swoops to her rescue, knocking Hook into the water. The captain then faces a long-time foe, the Crocodile, who has been after the captain since getting a taste of his hand.

The Indians celebrate when Peter returns with Tiger Lily. Wendy, envious of Peter's attention to the princes, leaves early and returns to Hangman's Tree, Peter's hideout.

Never Smile At A Crocodile

A Pirate's Life

In the meantime, Captain Hook has captured Tinker Bell, promising the pixie he will free her and eliminate Wendy if she will show him where Peter lives. Tink obliges, but Hook, going back on his word, imprisons her in a glass lantern before leaving to destroy Peter Pan.

At Hangman's Tree, Wendy convinces her brothers to return with her to London. The Lost Boys decide to accompany the Darlings, but as the group leaves the hideout, Hook's pirates capture them. Hook leaves a gift for Peter marked "From Wendy."

Aboard Hook's ship, the pirates tell Wendy and the boys they must either become pirates or walk the plank. When Wendy says Peter Pan will save them, Hook boasts that the "gift" he left in the hideout is a bomb. Hearing this from her lantern prison, Tinker Bell is enraged. She shatters the lantern and flits away to save Peter.

From the direction of Peter's hideout, a mighty explosion rends the air, and Hook makes Wendy walk the plank. But just before she hits the water, Peter soars in to save her. He challenges Hook to a final duel. A wild battle rages between the pirates and Peter and his friends are victorious. Hook gets knocked into the sea and tries once more to flee from the Crocodile.

Tinker Bell covers the ship with pixie dust and Peter takes the helm, setting sail for London.

Your Mother And Mine

Following The Leader

George and Mary Darling arrive home from the party and find Wendy asleep at the window. She awakens and tells them about her adventure, pointing to a gossamer ship sailing across the moon. Her father's expression softens, and he says, ''You know, I have the strangest feeling I've seen that ship before — when I was very young.''

Second Star To The Right

Following The Leader

Words by WINSTON HIBLER and TED SEARS
Music by OLIVER WALLACE

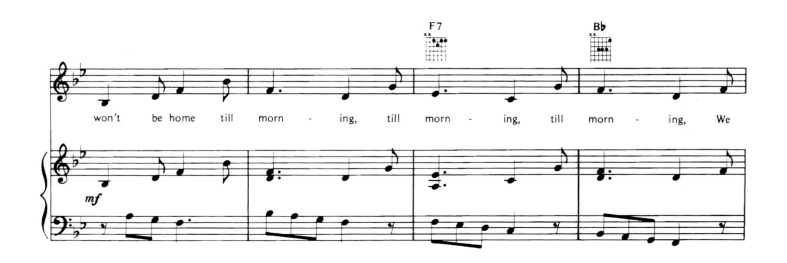

way with a tee - dle ee dum a tee - dle ee dō tee
ay, oh, a tee - dle ee dum a tee - dle ee dō tee

day. We're day. Oh a

tee - dle ee dum a tee - dle ee dō tee day.

What Made The Red Man Red?

Words by SAMMY CAHN
Music by SAMMY FAIN

Never Smile At A Crocodile

Words by JACK LAWRENCE
Music by FRANK CHURCHILL

A Pirate's Life

Words by ED PENNER
Music by OLIVER WALLACE

Your Mother And Mine

Words by SAMMY CAHN
Music by SAMMY FAIN